Therac 25

THERAC 25

ADAM PETTLE

Therac 25
first published 2000 by
Scirocco Drama
An imprint of J. Gordon Shillingford Publishing Inc.
© 2000 Adam Pettle
Reprinted 2006, 2013, 2018

Moonshadow words and music by Cat Stevens © 1970, Cat Music Ltd.

Scirocco Drama Series Editor: Glenda MacFarlane
Cover design by Doowah Design Inc.
Author photo by Geneviève Steele

Printed and bound in Canada on 100% post-consumer recycled paper.

We acknowledge the financial support of the Manitoba Arts Council and The Canada
Council for the Arts for our publishing program.

Production inquiries should be addressed to:
Charles Northcote
140 Wolfrey Avenue
Toronto, ON M4K 1L3
phone (416) 466-4929

Canadian Cataloguing in Publication Data

Pettle, Adam, 1973-
    Therac 25

A play.
ISBN 1-896239-70-6

    I. Title.
PS8581.E858T44 2000 C812'.6 C00-901159-5
PR9199.3.P455T44 2000

J. Gordon Shillingford Publishing
P.O. Box 86, RPO Corydon Avenue, Winnipeg, MB Canada R3M 3S3

To Mom, Dad and Jordan

Acknowledgements

First and always, my family. Dr. Ian Witterick, Dr. Paul Walfish, Melissa Vale, Dr. Brierly, the staff of the Princess Margaret Hospital, Kathryn Edgett, Fred and Caitlan. The Steele family, Judy Leigh Johnson, Andrew Joyce, John Cleland, Therese Zarb, Amer Diab, Trisha Welbourn, Alan Lyons, Andrew West, Maureen Labonte, J.M. Delpe, Ryan Rogerson, Burgandy Code. Ingrid Doucet, Geneviève Steele, Michael Kelar, Helen Zuckerman, Jason Long, Sarah Teitel, Charles Northcote, Joris Jarsky, The Canadian Stage Company, The Factory Theatre, Eastern Front Theatre, CBC Radio, Dalhousie University Theatre Department, The National Theatre School of Canada and The Canada Council for the Arts.

A special thank you to Iris Turcott and Jay Teitel.

Playwright's Note

It's July 15, 1995, and I'm back in the hospital—radioactive iodine therapy, cancer treatment's answer to solitary confinement. Why did I write this play? I wrote it to survive days like this. I wrote it for my Bubie Ruthie, the first person I ever knew with cancer. She battled advanced breast cancer for ten years, never letting the pain in her bones stop her from flipping ma-jong tiles or preparing Wednesday night spaghetti. I wrote it for Aunty Sharon and for my Uncle Irv, for Mrs. Nurenberg and Lise D'lille. I wrote it not only for those who have passed on to other journeys, but for all those who remain in Therac corridors everywhere. People that are not just statistics in flimsy pamphlets or black numbers on manila envelopes, but individuals with brilliant minds and raging spirits, with awe-inspiring courage and beautiful children.

Adam Pettle

Adam Pettle

Adam Pettle was born and raised in Toronto. His first play, *Therac 25* (Scirocco Drama, 2000), has received numerous productions across the country and has been adapted for CBC Radio. His play *Zadie's Shoes* (Scirocco Drama, 2001) premiered at Factory Theatre in 2001 and was subsequently picked up by Mirvish Productions and ran at the Wintergarden Theatre beginning in March 2002. *Sunday Father* premiered in 2002 and was published by Scirocco in 2003. Adam is currently the playwright-in-residence at the Canadian Stage Company.

Production History

Therac 25 premiered at the 1995 Atlantic Theatre Festival, Halifax, with the following creative team:

MOIRA.. Geneviève Steele
ALAN... Adam Pettle

Directed by Jean Morpugo
Stage Manager: Marcel Boulet

The Toronto premiere of *Therac 25* was produced by Slide Theatre and performed at the Tarragon Extra Space as part of the 1997 Summerworks Festival with the following team:

MOIRA..Kristen Thomson
ALAN... Adam Pettle
TECHNICIAN ....Sarah Teitel

Directed by Jordan Pettle
Set and Costume design by Vikki Anderson
Lighting and Sound design by Angela De Rocha
Stage Manager: Shauna Jansen

Scene One

A radiation treatment vault, the Princess Margaret Hospital.

MOIRA (24) walks into the radiation vault with a TECHNICIAN. The TECHNICIAN sits MOIRA on the treatment table and adjusts MOIRA's head, lining it up with the place where the radiation beams will appear. The TECHNICIAN then walks out of the vault and we hear the lead door slam behind her. From the booth we hear the TECHNICIAN's voice.

TECHNICIAN: Are you ready?

MOIRA: I can't wait.

TECHNICIAN: Hold still now, Moira. *(The whirr of the machine starts up.)* Electron cobalt treatment three, go.

There is a high-pitched buzzing sound as thin red laser beams appear in the shape of a cross and disappear into the top of MOIRA's head. After a beat, MOIRA closes her eyes and Cat Stevens' song Moonshadow *begins to play quietly. The song lasts for a few seconds and then we return to the buzz of the machine. The buzz then shuts off and we hear the voice of the TECHNICIAN from the booth:*

Good girl. You're done now. *(MOIRA does not move.)* We'll see you tomorrow.

MOIRA nods gently, then slowly gets off the table.

Scene Two

A waiting room, the Princess Margaret Hospital.
Early in the morning of the following day.

ALAN (22), sits in the waiting room. He has a
black, bound journal in his lap; he is trying to
write. After a beat or two, MOIRA enters the
waiting room. She grabs a Reader's Digest
and sits down in a chair, feigning interest in the
magazine. There is a long silence.

ALAN: It feels like junior hours at the golf course.

MOIRA: Pardon me?

ALAN: You know, the two hours before dawn when the
             junior members are actually allowed to use their
             memberships.

MOIRA: I hate golf.

ALAN: Me too. *(Pause.)* What year is it?

MOIRA: What?

ALAN: The *Digest*.

MOIRA: Oh. *(Checking the cover.)* Eighty-four.

ALAN: A fine year. The Summer Games in L.A., the
             arrival of *E.T.* ...Christ! That's ten years ago alr...
             Now why would they want us to read articles
             from ten years ago? We're cancer patients, not
             historians.

MOIRA: *E.T.* was released in '82... I was ten.

ALAN: Are you sure? No, wait, is... I thought *Chariots of Fire* won in—

MOIRA: I'm sure.

ALAN: I'm Alan.

MOIRA: Moira.

ALAN: So, where's your...?

MOIRA: On my mind.

ALAN: And what number treatment is this?

MOIRA: Nine.

ALAN: Of?

MOIRA: Twenty-five.

ALAN: Hey! Me too. I've got two today.

MOIRA: Yum.

ALAN: Yeah. You know, I wrote a limerick about two-treatment days.

MOIRA: Are you a poet?

ALAN: No. It's my first limerick and I'm not Irish. So... would you...? *(He motions to the journal.)*

MOIRA: Go for it.

ALAN: *(Flipping through his journal, finding poem, and reading:)*
           "O'Lucky Day.
           Two-treatment day.
           One at nine, one at three.
           To spend the day any other way,
           would be no fun, you see.

O'Lucky Day,
Two-treatment day—
twice the wait,
double the hate.
Heat…
Sleep…
Heat…
Sleep…
O'Lucky Day today!"

    ALAN starts slipping into a bad Irish accent:

"The sun is shining,
the birds will sing,
the mouth will dry,
the neck will sting.
O'Lucky Day,
two-treatment day,
will you go the fuck away!"

    Beat.

So?

MOIRA: That's not a limerick.

ALAN: Oh. Well I…I was playing with the traditional form, y'know…trying to release a greater sense of urgency throughout—

MOIRA: Are you trying to pick me up?

ALAN: What?! No, I mean, no! Christ, I've never even tried in a bar, I mean I just never know what to say, and in a waiting room at the Princess Margaret I think I'd really be out of my league. Shit! *(Grabbing his journal.)* That could be my book: "One Hundred and One Lines to Pick Up a Cancer Patient." *(He begins writing the idea down in his journal.)*

    Pause.

MOIRA: "Hey, baby! Want to go for some platinum injections?"

ALAN: *(Laughing.)* "You know, ah, I don't want to brag, but I've got the lowest white blood cell count in this place."

MOIRA: "I don't know if anyone has ever told you this, but you've got the most scannable skull I have ever..."

TECHNICIAN: *(Over an intercom.)* Mr. Feldman to Vault Forty-one. Mr. Feldman.

ALAN: That's me.

MOIRA: I guess.

ALAN: *(Getting his stuff together.)* What are you doing this afternoon?

MOIRA: I have chemo at eleven-thirty.

ALAN: You're doing both! *Mon Dieu.*

MOIRA: Just for another week. Then my cycle is over.

ALAN: Well, do you have plans after chemo? Another one for the book.

MOIRA: Vomiting.

ALAN: Can I join you?

MOIRA: You *are* trying to pick me up.

ALAN: I'm just... It's just that I have eight hours in between my two treatments... If I go home, I'll fall asleep in front of *Geraldo*, if I stay down here, I'll wander from coffee shop to coffee shop sipping herbal tea and writing bad limericks. We could go for coffee in the four-star cafeteria.

MOIRA: Why would you want to go out with me? I'm... I'm bald.

ALAN: I'm Jewish.

MOIRA: Imagine what our kids would look like.

ALAN: My grandfather. What do you say?

MOIRA: You should go in already.

ALAN: Ah, I like to keep him waiting.

MOIRA: Who?

ALAN: The T-25, that... That monster that treats me. What do you say?

MOIRA: I'll meet you in the caf at twelve-thirty.

ALAN: Great! Have a good... Do you say "Have a good chemo?"

MOIRA: No.

> *ALAN walks out of the room, MOIRA closes her eyes and puts her face in her hands. ALAN re-enters the room.*

ALAN: You did say twel—?

MOIRA: What?

ALAN: Sorry, I... Are you... How are you feeling?

MOIRA: Don't say that.

ALAN: I know—the world's worst question and yet I ask it; it's just—

MOIRA: No! It's not a joke. If you want to know me, you can never ask me that, it's a rule, you understand?

ALAN: Yes. *(Pause.)* Do you still want to meet me for coffee?

MOIRA: Maybe I'll be there and maybe I won't.

ALAN exits. The lights fade.

Scene Three

> *ALAN sits in the cafeteria drinking a tea, anxiously looking to the door. After a few beats MOIRA enters the cafeteria and approaches ALAN's table, gingerly.*

ALAN: You came.

MOIRA: I decided to forgive you.

ALAN: Thanks. How was—?

MOIRA: Don't ask. *(She takes a pill out of her bag and washes it down with her bottled water.)* So when was your diagnosis?

ALAN: Late August.

MOIRA: And what was… ?

ALAN: Oh, ah… a tumour on my thyroid gland which was removed two weeks later, along with eleven cancerous lymph nodes and the nerve attached to my left vocal cord, hence the Tom Waits impersonation.

MOIRA: Yeah, I was going to ask you about that.

ALAN: The tumour was wrapped around the nerve, which was a surprise to me and to Dr. Brierly. He spent an hour during my surgery deciding whether to remove the nerve or—

MOIRA: Will you excuse me for a second? *(Before the question is answered, she is up and out.)*

ALAN: *(To himself:)* I think she's gone to throw up. Is it the chemo, or the smell of the meatloaf? Or me? I wish I could... Maybe she wants me to go out there. I can't. Christ, you know most people pick the Second Cup for their first date, maybe an early movie and a bite afterwards... We are not most people.

MOIRA: *(Re-entering the cafeteria.)* Sorry. What were you saying?

ALAN: I... I don't remember.

MOIRA: Oh. We were talking about your surgery.

ALAN: Right. Ah, gone: thyroid, parathyroid, eleven lymph nodes—enough for a soccer team—the nerve attached to vocal cord, gained a...a new pair of eyes. You know, I was hoping they would do something about this nose, but...not enough OR time, I guess. Cutbacks, you know?

MOIRA: A new pair of eyes?

ALAN: Did you have surgery?

MOIRA: No. It's inoperable. Like your nose. Why?

ALAN: Nothing. *(Pause.)* So, what do you want to be when you grow up?

MOIRA: Alive.

ALAN: I... I hear there's good money in that.

MOIRA: I was in my third year of Sociology. I was thinking about social work.

ALAN: You *are* thinking about social work.

MOIRA: Whatever. Do you know what time it is?

ALAN: Twenty after one.

MOIRA:	I've got a few minutes.
ALAN:	Are you getting picked up?
MOIRA:	Yeah. Chris…my boyfriend…is coming to get me at one-thirty.
ALAN:	Great. Have you been with him long?
MOIRA:	About a year. He's studying Political Science at Concordia; he's just in for his Christmas break. Do you need a lift somewhere? I'm sure—
ALAN:	Oh, no thanks, I've got my car.
MOIRA:	Ooooh, he's got a car.
ALAN:	Yeah, she's a '79 Gremlin. It was my high school graduation present.
MOIRA:	A Gremlin?
ALAN:	Yeah, well, I didn't do that well in high school. Do you drive?
MOIRA:	I do, but not lately. I mean, you know what they say about morphine and driving.
ALAN:	Well, you should give me your number. I mean, I'm coming down here every day, I'd be happy to give you a lift if you—
MOIRA:	That'd be great. Pen?
ALAN:	I've got one.
MOIRA:	Of course the poet has a pen.

> She starts writing her phone number down and laughing.

| ALAN: | What? |
| MOIRA: | I was just thinking… I wonder what's more |

distasteful: the chemo, or being driven to it in a
Gremlin?

ALAN: Eh! Enough with the car. Here, I'm going to give
             you mine, too. *(He writes down his number, starts
             to hand it to her, then pulls it back.)* Now no crank
             calls, OK?

MOIRA: I promise.

Scene Four

> *ALAN's house/MOIRA's house. A phone rings. A pool of light comes up on ALAN at home.*

ALAN: Hello.

> *A pool of light comes up on MOIRA who has a washcloth draped over her head.*

MOIRA: Hi.

ALAN: Oh. Hi.

MOIRA: I wasn't expecting to use your number already... tonight, I mean, it's just that I... I...mean...

ALAN: *(Simultaneously with "mean":)* No, I'm really glad you did.

MOIRA: I wanted to thank you for coffee today.

ALAN: No problem. How are you feeling?

> *MOIRA hangs up the phone.*

Oh shit!

> *ALAN searches his pockets for her number, and on finding it, calls her back. The phone rings in MOIRA's house. She just looks at it. After six or seven rings, MOIRA finally picks up the phone.*

MOIRA: What did I tell you?!

ALAN: Moira, I am so sorry. It is just that you...you sounded a bit down.

MOIRA: We've known each other for ten hours, and already he knows my moods, I love that about us.

ALAN: No, I... I don't know.

            Pause.

MOIRA: I just watched *Montel Williams.*

ALAN: The black guy?

MOIRA: The bald guy.

ALAN: Maybe that's it.

MOIRA: What?

ALAN: Why you sound down.

MOIRA: Yeah, it was a pretty depressing episode.

ALAN: Oh?

MOIRA: "Spontaneous remissions, miracle recoveries from incurable diseases."

ALAN: And you sat through that?

MOIRA: I like his hair. What have you been up to all evening?

ALAN: Eating cornchips and masturbating.

MOIRA: Lovely. Is this something you do often?

ALAN: Yes. And you?

MOIRA: What?

ALAN: Do you masturbate?

MOIRA: No.

ALAN: Bullshit.

MOIRA: What do you mean, bullshit?

ALAN: Everybody mastur—

MOIRA: Just because you are the Frito Lay goalie-pulling
            champion does not mean... Lately it just seems
            to be one of those hobbies that I have very little
            time for.

ALAN: Really? Seems like just the opposite for me.

MOIRA: Isn't it nicer to have...just to have someone hold
            you?

            Pause.

ALAN: Yeah.

            Pause.

MOIRA: Are you masturbating right now?

ALAN: No! It's not a chronic condition, y'know.

MOIRA: You should try your opposite hand some time,
            feels like someone else is doing it.

ALAN: Really? Did a friend tell you that?

MOIRA: *(Holding the phone away.)* What's that, Ma? My
            mom's got to use the phone.

ALAN: Oh. Ah... OK...um... Do you need a lift down
            tomorrow?

MOIRA: No thanks. My mom's going to take me.

ALAN: Oh. So, will I see you tomorrow?

MOIRA: Maybe. Have sweet dreams.

ALAN: Yeah. You too. *Bonne nuit. (He starts to hang up the
            phone.)*

MOIRA: Wait. I have a high-grade pineal tumour that resembles medulloblastoma. Goodnight.

MOIRA hangs up.

Scene Five

MOIRA is lying on a treatment cot waiting to be administered her daily dose of chemotherapy. There is an IV bag hanging beside her, but she is not hooked up yet. She is reading a National Enquirer magazine. ALAN enters dressed in a surgical mask, gloves, stethoscope, and lab coat.

ALAN: *(Putting on a latex glove and doing his best mad German doctor impersonation:)* Moira! Moira!

MOIRA: *(Putting paper down.)* What are you doing here?

ALAN: The woman at Patient Information told me your chemo was in here.

MOIRA: She shouldn't have.

ALAN: What are you reading?

MOIRA: *King Lear.*

ALAN: Really? I didn't know Burt Reynolds was in that one.

MOIRA: What are you doing here?

ALAN: I haven't seen you in a few days, I...I thought I could keep you company.

MOIRA: This is not really a company thing.

ALAN: Oh. Do you want me to leave?

MOIRA: I'm still deciding.

ALAN: Have you had your... Sorry, I don't know how this works.

MOIRA: They have to test my blood to make sure it's OK to poison it.

ALAN: Right. What are we having today, anyway?

MOIRA: It's a lovely zinc flan, not currently on the menu.

ALAN: Special.

MOIRA: Yes. And you?

ALAN: No thanks, I ate.

MOIRA: No, I mean have you had your treatment yet?

ALAN: Yeah, I just came from there.

MOIRA: How was it?

ALAN: Oh Christ, you missed quite the rhubarb this morning.

MOIRA: Rhubarb?

ALAN: Well, there was almost a fight in the waiting room.

MOIRA: Fuck off.

ALAN: I swear to God.

MOIRA: Between?

ALAN: Between the praying mantis and the—

MOIRA: The praying mantis?

ALAN: You know, the forty-something Portuguese woman who sits in the corner and prays out loud until she's called in?

MOIRA: I know the one.

ALAN: Well, it was between her and the nose.

MOIRA: The nose?

ALAN: *(Bending his nose.)* The nose.

MOIRA: Not her!

ALAN: Yes, see the mantis was sitting in the corner pray-
            ing as per usual, y'know, Portuguese Hail Marys
            out loud, interrupted by only the occasional
            moan. You know the drill?

MOIRA: Yes.

ALAN: And so in walks the nose, and she's...she's
            visibly upset.

MOIRA: I can't see why.

ALAN: No, I know. The woman's on like week four of
            having her nose burnt off, needless to say she
            doesn't have much patience. So, she sits down
            like two seats away from the mantis, because—
            between you and me—I think she's been wanting
            to get into it with her for a while. Anyway, she
            lasts about ten seconds until she leans over and
            goes: "Will you do us all a giant favour and
            please SHUT THE FUCK UP!"

MOIRA: No.

ALAN: Yeah, and the mantis stands up, not missing a
            beat, and goes: "'You can pick your friends, and
            you can pick your nose, but—"

MOIRA: *(Laughing.)* You are so full of shit.

ALAN: OK, it was slightly embellished. Do you mind if
            I...just hang out for a bit?

MOIRA: If you want to. All right.

ALAN takes off the stolen hospital garb and stuffs it under MOIRA's cot.

MOIRA: So, how's the circuit treating you?

ALAN: The circuit?

MOIRA: The eel-wrestling circuit.

ALAN: You know, for someone who doesn't partake, you seem to know more than a few allegories to describe—

MOIRA: Allegories?

ALAN: What? Is that the wrong word?

MOIRA: Dante's representation of hell in *The Divine Comedy* is an allegory, wrestling the eel is not.

ALAN: What is it, then?

MOIRA: A sin. *(Pause.)* So, I thought you were avoiding me.

ALAN: No, why?

MOIRA: Well, it's just… I haven't seen you in a week.

ALAN: I know; I've had really early appointments.

MOIRA: Oh. I thought maybe maybe you didn't want to hang around with someone who…who watches Montel.

ALAN: We all have our vices.

MOIRA: Yeah, and you've got a vice grip on your—

ALAN: Oh, y'know, can we please just let that die?

MOIRA: Actually, that's not the best allegory to use in here.

ALAN: I'm sorry. *(Pause.)* So can we?

MOIRA:	Can we what?
ALAN:	Drop the masturbation thing?
MOIRA:	Absolutely not.
ALAN:	Thank you.
MOIRA:	I've got to have something on you.
ALAN:	Why?
MOIRA:	Why? Because you caught me reading the *National Enquirer* and because...
ALAN:	Because?
MOIRA:	I don't let people in here.
ALAN:	Oh.
MOIRA:	Well, don't get smug.
ALAN:	I'm not smug.
MOIRA:	Just...don't. Where are they?
ALAN:	Who comes in to give you the—?
MOIRA:	You know, I really don't feel like talking any more.
ALAN:	Oh. OK. Do you want me to leave?
MOIRA:	No. Just...sit there and keep me company, OK?
ALAN:	OK.

Scene Six

> *A small Greek Orthodox church beside the hospital.*

MOIRA: Thanks for bringing me here. I haven't been in a church in three years.

ALAN: Wedding?

MOIRA: Christening.

ALAN: Oh, that's the *(Makes a flicking motion)* water ordeal, right?

MOIRA: Yeah. Oh, you guys don't get christened, do you?

ALAN: No. Just *(Makes a snipping motion by his crotch.)*

MOIRA: Hey! Get your hands away from there.

> *Pause.*

ALAN: Happy halfway home.

MOIRA: What?

ALAN: Treatment number thirteen, *c'est finis!*

MOIRA: Why do you do that?

ALAN: What?

MOIRA: That French thing at the end of your sentences.

ALAN: I didn't realize that I...

MOIRA: If we were married that would be one of those

things that would secretly drive me crazy and eventually force me into an adulterous affair.

ALAN: *C'est dommage!* I think the way that you stare at my hairline when I'm speaking would have me banging the maid long before you had a chance to—

MOIRA: Banging the maid?

ALAN: Yes, bang—

MOIRA: Is that what sex is with you? Banging?

ALAN: Well, there is some banging involved. Do you think this is the place to be discussing this?

MOIRA: No. *(Pause.)* If you'd said I would be nailing the maid, then we'd—

ALAN: Oh. Nice. Crucifixion jokes, we are in big trouble.

MOIRA: Oh, you're right, I shouldn't mock God, make … make jokes about Jesus, I should be grateful for all this great luck I've been having.

ALAN: Moira.

MOIRA: I'm sorry, God, please don't give me locusts or… or a brain tumour, or—

ALAN: Moira, please—

MOIRA: Excuse me! I'm talking to God. And when I die, please take care of mommy and daddy and my dog Suzie, and my uncle Bert, even though he smells like cheese and gives me bad touches in the furnace room, and grandma and grandpa in heaven—

ALAN: Moira.

MOIRA: And my tight-assed friend Alan! Amen.

Pause.

ALAN: Do you ever wonder why everyone cries when they're born?

MOIRA: No, I never have.

ALAN: But I mean, not everyone cries when they die, right? At least not on TV.

MOIRA: No, they don't. I think you're on to something, Nietzsche.

ALAN: Why do you do that? I'm trying to talk to you.

MOIRA: And I'm trying to tell you I don't want to.

ALAN: I'm not talking about dying tomorrow, it's a long way off, for both of us, but it is inevitable, and ... and I think we could talk about it.

MOIRA: I don't want to talk about it.

ALAN: Because?

MOIRA: Because.

ALAN: Because you're afraid of it?

MOIRA: It's unknown.

ALAN: Yes. And so is tomorrow.

MOIRA: Are you afraid of tomorrow?

ALAN: Yes. My grandmother's bringing me potato kugel, she thinks it will be easy on my throat.

MOIRA: I'm afraid I won't be here.

ALAN: Me too. But I'm more afraid of the kugel.

MOIRA: Your top three.

ALAN: What?

MOIRA: Your top three biggest regrets if you die tomor-
            row, not that it's going to happen.

ALAN: OK. Ah…playing catch with my son.

MOIRA: Or daughter.

ALAN: Or daughter.

MOIRA: You're like Pete Rose.

ALAN: What?

MOIRA: Pete Rose took his son to the World Series and
            left his daughter at home. He said, "She wouldn't
            have been interested in coming."

ALAN: That is disgu… I am not like Pete Rose, I would
            love to play catch with my daughter.

MOIRA: I hope so.

ALAN: As long as she didn't throw like a girl.

MOIRA: Fucking pig!

ALAN: Shhh.

MOIRA: Fuck.

ALAN: Moira.

MOIRA: Fuck, fuck, fuck! Fuck! Piss! Fuck! Shit!

ALAN: (Simultaneously with "Piss!") This is the most
            intelligent conversation I've had in a while.

MOIRA: Fucking A!

ALAN: Moira.

MOIRA: How can you possibly be up-tight?

ALAN: I am not up-tight. There's nothing wrong with
            having a little, some, tact.

MOIRA:	I guess you can. I guess that's one of the differences between us.
ALAN:	What's that supposed to mean?
MOIRA:	What are the chances of your cancer recurring, what?! Seventy-five percent it won't.
ALAN:	Yes! And you've got a good chance, too. I looked up meduloblastoma, it's treatable! You've got a really good shot at beating this thing!
MOIRA:	Why don't you go beat your thing?

Pause.

ALAN:	You know I... I watched *The Flintstones* this morning, six a.m. on YTV, I couldn't sleep, but I did have this thought. Moira, lis... If you had a six-year-old child and he had supernatural strength, would you give him a club?
MOIRA:	Why make jokes? Always! Christ, I'd divorce you for that, too. I think I'm going to throw up.
ALAN:	It wasn't that bad.
MOIRA:	No, I'm going to throw up.
ALAN:	Oh shit. Is there...is there anything I can do for you?
MOIRA:	Hold my hair back.
ALAN:	No, some... Some water...something to...
MOIRA:	There was a bowl with some water in the lobby.
ALAN:	That's the holy water.
MOIRA:	So?!
ALAN:	So, I don't know if we're supposed to... All right, look, stay here.

MOIRA looks at him as if to say, "Where am I going to go?" ALAN runs out into the lobby of the church. MOIRA begins to sing Moonshadow *to herself. After a beat or two, she begins to vomit.*

ALAN: *(Running back in.)* Moira, Moira, do you want this?

MOIRA: Better late than never.

ALAN hesitantly holds out the bowl.

Put it down!

MOIRA retches into the bowl.

ALAN: Ah...is there anything else I can do for you?

MOIRA: Sing *Moonshadow.*

ALAN: What?

MOIRA: Cat Stevens, *Moonshadow,* sing it.

ALAN: Moira, I... I

MOIRA: What?!

ALAN: I don't know it.

MOIRA continues to retch. ALAN stands behind her in quiet desperation. Lights fade.

Scene Seven

> ALAN and MOIRA stand in two separate pools
> of light.

MOIRA: I read this story—

ALAN: What else would God possibly want that bowl
           used for?

MOIRA: I read this story about a woman who was terr—

ALAN: I had a Cat Stevens tape once, why the fuck didn't
           I listen to it?

MOIRA: I read this story about a woman who was terrified
           of losing her breast to a mastectomy. When she
           asked her husband what it would mean to him,
           he said: "All it would mean is that I could put my
           hand even closer to your heart." What a guy to
           have. What a bond to have.

ALAN: I should have held her head.

MOIRA: I'd rather have my tit.

Scene Eight

> *MOIRA is playing in a park by her family's house. ALAN approaches, cold and coughing.*

MOIRA: Hi.

ALAN: Hi.

> *He sits down on the park bench.*

MOIRA: You didn't have any trouble finding it?

ALAN: No. *(Pause.)* Are you cold?

MOIRA: A bit. You?

ALAN: I'm fucking freezing.

MOIRA: Oh.

> *MOIRA goes to rub his shoulders. ALAN shies away.*

ALAN: How's Chris?

MOIRA: Good. He's calling later tonight.

ALAN: Oh. *(He starts to cough.)*

MOIRA: You sound like shit.

ALAN: Thank you.

MOIRA: Are you taking that liquid codeine they prescribed for you?

ALAN: No.

MOIRA: What are you waiting for?

ALAN: Until I absolutely can't take the pain any more.

MOIRA: Who are you, Gandhi?

ALAN: No, look, I wanted to apologize for the—

MOIRA: Let's fly.

ALAN: Pardon?

MOIRA: Let's fly.

ALAN: Sorry?

MOIRA: On those swings over there.

ALAN: I can't.

MOIRA: Pardon?

ALAN: I can't swing.

MOIRA: You can't swing?

ALAN: I can't...no. It's the leg pump, I could never get
             the leg pump; my friends would always be on
             either side of me, rapping with God and St. Peter
             and I'd be hopelessly pumping two feet off the—
             (ALAN *begins to cough*.)

MOIRA: Pathetic. So very...

             MOIRA puts her hand on ALAN's back.

ALAN: (*Getting up and moving away.*) No, I can't.

MOIRA: Can't what?

ALAN: Be touched.

MOIRA: I'm sorry I—

ALAN: I'm sorry I… I tried to tell you. It's just that since September, since my surgery, I… Oh, fuck.

MOIRA: What?

ALAN: I can't…

MOIRA: Alan?

ALAN: I can't…I have days when I can't be touched, not by hands, not by drugs, not even a hug from my mother. And I need you to know that it's not your hands that are making me nauseous, it's this body… How am I supposed to have a relationship? How am I supposed to explain why I'm crying for the ninth night in a row? And it's not that *The Lion King* is a terribly tragic film, it's that I've checked out of the movie and instead I'm watching myself… You know, I don't even like it when someone holds my hand.

MOIRA: How about a blow job?

ALAN: You offering?

MOIRA: Yes. I could use a little something to take my mind off of things.

         They share a laugh. She runs her finger along his nose; he pulls away a little, but tries to stay with her. She moves to hug him.

         It's OK.

         She hugs him. He tries to be held for a moment, then pushes her away.

ALAN: No! I can't. Didn't you hear me? That's my rule, OK?

MOIRA: I think I'd better go.

ALAN: Moira, please.

MOIRA begins walking out of the park, staggering a little.

Moira?

Suddenly MOIRA grabs the back of her neck then falls onto the snow, convulsing in a seizure.

Oh my God!

Lights fade.

Scene Nine

> *A hospital room. MOIRA sits in a hospital bed,*
> *hooked to an IV. She is staring out the window,*
> *ALAN enters.*

MOIRA: I don't want you here.

ALAN: Moira, please.

MOIRA: I want you to leave.

ALAN: Just—

MOIRA: It's going to be really fucking embarassing if I have to call Security—for both of us—so I'm asking you once more to leave.

ALAN: I can't just leave things like this.

MOIRA: Which part of that didn't you fucking understand? Go away!

ALAN: No—you—just let me apologize, OK, and then I'll leave.

MOIRA: Oh! I get it! You think this is your fault. This is a guilt visit. You won't be able to live with yourself thinking you caused the seizure that broke the camel's back.

ALAN: *(Simultaneously with "live:")* That's not what I'm saying. I just need to talk to you.

MOIRA: You need to talk to me?

ALAN: Yes.

MOIRA: What could there possibly be to talk about? Now get the fuck out and don't come back.

ALAN: It's not that easy.

MOIRA: If you ever cared a moment about me, you'll walk out that door and never come back.

ALAN looks at her for a moment then walks out of the room. There is a long beat of silence. Then, from outside the door we hear:

ALAN: "I'm being followed by a moonshadow, moonshadow, moonshadow. I'm leaping and hopping on a moonshadow, moonshadow, moonshadow…"

He has some trouble remembering the words:

"And if I ever lose my eyes, lose my eyes, if I lose. And if I ever lose my eyes, oh way hey hey hey hey hey hey hey hey, I won't have to see again."

Pause.

MOIRA: Keep going.

ALAN: "And if I ever lose my legs, lose my power, cannot walk, and if I ever lose my legs, oh way hey hey hey hey hey hey hey hey, I'm coming on a moonshadow."

MOIRA: Come in here.

ALAN re-enters the room.

ALAN: I…

MOIRA: Next verse.

ALAN: What? I only learned one…

MOIRA: It's a joke.

Pause.

ALAN: What's happening?

MOIRA: I told you that my tumour resembled meduloblastoma, but what makes it different is that it can travel through the spinal fluid to other parts of the brain and…mine has.

ALAN: What does that mean?

MOIRA: That I'm going to die.

ALAN: When?

MOIRA: Soon.

ALAN: Is there anything I can do?

> *MOIRA shakes her head, but then it slowly turns into a nod. She looks at him, reaches down and touches his nose. ALAN does not pull away. MOIRA runs her hand down his face, and then takes his hand and puts it on her chest.*

Moira?

MOIRA: Yes.

ALAN: How are you feeling?

MOIRA: I'm scared.

> *Lights fade to black.*

The End.